Other books by Bob Kamm

The Superman Syndrome: *How the Information Age Threatens Your Future and What You Can Do About It,* 2000

Real Fatherhood: *The Path of Lyrical Parenting,* 2002

Lyric Heart, *Poems and other Musings,* 2007

Love

Over

60

later the hour, sweeter the moment...

BY

Bob Kamm

authorHOUSE®

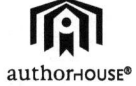

AuthorHouse™
1663 Liberty Drive
Bloomington, IN 47403
www.authorhouse.com
Phone: 1-800-839-8640

© 2011 Bob Kamm. All rights reserved.

No part of this book may be reproduced, stored in a retrieval system, or transmitted by any means without the written permission of the author.

First published by AuthorHouse 3/21/2011

ISBN: 978-1-4520-8475-6 (e)
ISBN: 978-1-4520-8474-9 (sc)

Library of Congress Control Number: 2010914550

Printed in the United States of America

This book is printed on acid-free paper.

Because of the dynamic nature of the Internet, any Web addresses or links contained in this book may have changed since publication and may no longer be valid. The views expressed in this work are solely those of the author and do not necessarily reflect the views of the publisher, and the publisher hereby disclaims any responsibility for them.

for
Annie

Contents

Introduction: How Andrea and Bob Met and What Happened ix

The Choice 1
The Cradle Won't Fall 5
Bright Form 7
Crazy Beautiful 9
Sixty-Sex 14
The Unmeasure of Love 15
Divine Breath 16
Sweet Phrasing 17
Behind the Dream 18
New Mosaic 19
Beast on Beast 20
Pretty Good Eaters 22
Force of Nature 24
Complements 25
The Chair 28
Our Island 30
Callings 32
Unbounded 36
The Temple 39
Wishes 44
Shoes 46
Window Treatments, Cockroaches and Cat-Chicken 49
Baggage and Truth 51
An End to Ordinary 53
Poems I'll Never Write for You 54

Fountains and Youth	56
A Saying of the Father	59
Sunlight and Shadows	62
The Sweetness	65
Short Selling	67
Singularity	69
Enough Already!	73
Dandelions, We	75
Love Doesn't Count	76
The Pointer	77
Four-Letter Love	84
Love Liberated	87
The Apprentice	88
Spoonin'	89
Church Whispers	91
Knowing and Knowing	92
There	94
Remedy	95
Half Moon	96
World-Walker	97
The Question	98
Summer in Autumn	99
July Skies	101
About the Author	103

Introduction:
How Andrea and Bob Met and What Happened

March, 2000: Chris, a petite but powerful Southern California business woman meets Bob while he is consulting to her organization. A few minutes into their first conversation, she is thinking, "He would he be perfect for my friend, Andrea!" But there's a catch, a big one. Both Andrea and Bob are married, not to mention the fact they live two hundred and fifty miles from each other.

July 7, 2007: Though Chris rarely ventures into the role of matchmaker, for seven and a-half years, she has been unable to shake the idea that Andrea and Bob belong together. Suddenly, on this day, it strikes her that even though they are still separated by two hundred and fifty miles, they are now both available. She swings into action. First, she reminds Andrea of "the man I've been telling you about for years who lives up north" and gives her a copy of Bob's recently published collection of poems, *Lyric Heart*. Andrea is captivated by the verses, thinking to herself, "What a good man this is." A dozen days later, she is out in the evening with Chris, who continues to talk up Bob. "Okay," Andrea says. "Do something!" That night, Chris sends Bob an email reminding him of "the wonderful woman I've been telling you about for years." She suggests the timing is right for "whatever it might become" and offers Andrea's email.

Friday morning, July 20, 2007: Bob, sixty years old, is a writer and business consultant specializing in leadership development and organizational change. He's been married twice and doesn't know if he'll ever find the love he's been seeking all his life. He has tried online dating for about six weeks but, given the swings from anticipation to disappointment, has come to call it "the bipolar express." He wakes up and, as is his custom, goes to check his email. There's a message from his friend, Chris. Bob feels the excitement and urgency in her words and thinks, "She's a very sharp cookie. This is worth pursuing." He immediately sends off a three hundred word email to Andrea, introducing himself and remarking, "Maybe Chris knows something."

Andrea is sixty-four, a Licensed Marriage and Family Therapist and Clinical Art Therapist. She's been married twice. She is hoping that she may yet have an even greater love than she has experienced, but doubtful it will come. However, she has written down what she dreams of in a man and has been carrying the list in her wallet. "A writer, a conscious man, sensitive, kind, tall, handsome in an ethnic sort of way, smart, funny, sexual." Suddenly, on this morning, during a break between clients, she receives an email from the man whose praises Chris has been singing. She already has his book so there is a check in the writer box. From the poems she has read so far, she knows he's sensitive and smart. From the picture on the back cover, she thinks he could be handsome, though he looks a little stocky. His email speaks of consciousness. It contains hints of other things, but is thoroughly appropriate. Very intriguing. She shoots back a message of similar length, remarking at the end, "Maybe Chris does know something." She also offers her phone number. Bob is still at his computer when Andrea's email comes through. Her words strike him as luminous, full of consciousness—a precious commodity in a man or woman in his experience. He picks up the phone. Their connection is immediate, powerful and deep. It flows. Forty-five minutes pass in a flash and Andrea has a client arriving. That night, Bob calls again but gets the answering machine. "I hope this doesn't seem too forward," he says, "but our conversation this morning was just so rich. It left me wanting more." A half-hour later, Andrea returns from dinner, listens and calls back. They're on the phone for two hours.

Saturday, Sunday, Monday, July 21-23, 2007: Andrea and Bob talk by phone two to three hours a day. They are loving each other's voices, rhythms and ways of expressing themselves. Their conversations range wide and deep—family, work, art, travel, books, ethics—and synchronicities abound.

They have both read a number of the same esoteric books on the psychology of relationships. Bob hears music in the background of Andrea's house and immediately identifies it. "You're listening to Eva Cassidy, right? I love her." Yes, Eva Cassidy…and her wonderful rendition of Sting's *Fields of Gold*.

And dogs. Bob hasn't had a dog since he was seven. Andrea has a silver Siberian husky named Sofie. Bob has always loved huskies…and the name Sophie. "I rescued her when she was eight months old," Andrea relates. So I named her after the movie, *Sophie's Choice*, but decided to spell it with an F…don't ask me why."

"I loved that movie!" Bob tells her. "But I've loved the name Sophie since childhood. I had a great aunt by that name. She had soft silver hair…like your silver dog. Go figure." Bob doesn't yet mention that he's been allergic to dogs most of his adult life, which is why he hasn't had one. But, "Hey," he thinks, "There are always antihistamines." Then he remembers drawing a dog's head from an art book when he was seven. It was a beautiful silver Siberian husky. He remembers the hours he spent carefully shading in the "mask" over the eyes typical of huskies. He also remembers thinking at the time, "This is the dog I'll have some day.

Bob has been to Peru five times since 1987. It has become a kind of spiritual home away from home and he has longed to share it with a woman he deeply loves. Andrea is an avid traveler. She has zip-lined in Costa Rica, visited the vineyards and cathedrals of Europe and the jungles of Southeast Asia. "I'm low maintenance," she says. I'd love to go to Peru with you."

Tuesday Evening, July 24, 2007: Bob and Andrea are already making plans to meet mid-way between their two locations in about two weeks. However, on this evening, Andrea says, "It's too bad you live so far away. I'm having a birthday party Friday night for my best girl friend."

Bob responds, "Are you asking me to dinner?"

Andrea answers, "Well, I guess I am."

Bob has spent a lot of time on the road. The prospect of a five-hour drive to meet Andrea doesn't faze him in the least. He double-checks his schedule. "Okay, I'm coming! Do you have a guest room where I can crash?"

"Yes, I do!"

That night, three more hours on the phone.

Wednesday, July 25, 2007: Suddenly, this connection has taken on a much weightier reality. Bob and Andrea are going to meet face to face in just a few days. Andrea expresses two concerns. She had planned to share the first with him when they were originally going to rendezvous for lunch half-way between their homes. Now, things are moving much faster. She puts it in writing in an email, so it will be totally clear. Her husband, Leonard, an architect, had a catastrophic stroke a dozen years earlier. The left side of his brain was largely wiped out. She is committed to caring for him the rest of his life. He is now in his early seventies and more like a child than a man. He understands most of what is said to him but struggles to speak more than a few words. She tried placing him in a care facility but was horrified by the conditions and treatment at even the premier institutions. His needs are simple—good food, clean clothes, a comfortable chair, regular hygiene care and a TV to show old movies. He can't engage in much more than a few minutes of interaction with others before his attention drifts back to Bogie and Bacall or any of the other many stars he loves from the black and white era. Andrea has a little room in back of her house. That's where Leonard lives…with his big screen TV. She assures Bob that she is available to him "mentally, emotionally and physically and will be legally before long." But she adds, "If you want to walk away, I'll understand." She has done some dating in the past few years and men have walked away for this very reason

As soon as he reads her email, Bob picks up the phone and calls. "This is not a problem," he says. "I'm glad you told me about it up front like this. The whole thing speaks volumes about your character. In fact, it only makes me want to get down there faster to meet you."

That brings up Andrea's second concern, which she voices now. "Bob, we have this great connection. But what if the *'it'* isn't there. I mean, physical attraction is a reality. All we have is pictures of each other…and Chris's descriptions. I think we both want passion. What if it's not there?"

Bob has had a similar thought, and says, "Well, let's just trust this. If the *'it'* isn't there, we'll be great friends at the very least."

Wednesday and Thursday, July 25, 26, 2007: Three hours on the phone each day, sharing specifics about their respective work days, the ills and joys of getting older, childhood memories, parenting sorrows and satisfactions, real estate deals, thoughts about retirement.

Friday, July 27th, 2007: As he's making the two-hundred and fifty mile drive toward Andrea's home, they are on the phone constantly until Andrea guides Bob off Pacific Coast Highway to her street. It's a charming older neighborhood with the cottages clustered together cheek by jowl. He enters her narrow driveway, crammed in between a block wall on one side and a beautiful natural stone wall on the other. He sees her through the large living room window, still holding the phone to her ear. She is tall, beautiful and womanly as she moves toward the open front door. He gets out of the car, squeezes between it and the stone wall, gingerly focuses on the latch of the wrought iron gate and swings it open. He looks up and smiles, hesitating for just a second. Andrea takes in that big smile and his eyes and an endearing bit of tentativeness as he moves almost in slow motion up the path. She thinks, "His face is joyful and so alive and, thank God, he's not stocky at all. He's tall!"

They meet at the threshold. He takes in her face, the finely sculpted nose, exquisite cheekbones. He looks down into her deep brown eyes. She looks up into his deep brown eyes. They reach for each other expecting a warm hug but immediately fall into a kiss that goes on and on and on—something neither of them saw coming. It is tender, curious, probing and passionate. The day is hot. Their bodies are hotter. The 'it'? Oh yeah, the 'it'. The 'it' lives!

When they break for air, Bob gives Andrea an authentic hand-woven belt from Peru

Andrea says, "Until I looked in your eyes, I wasn't sure I'd give this to you. But here." She hands him a card. Bob opens it. In it, she has written, "I thought I'd never find you."

They hug and cry.. "We've come home," he says.

For the rest of the afternoon, they hug, kiss, laugh, sway to Eva Cassidy singing *Fields of Gold* and *Over the Rainbow*, and prepare dinner. Actually, Andrea has most of it handled but Bob does make the salad. He's good at slicing avocados—an important skill for any California man.

The guests arrive at seven—two couples, including Andrea's best girlfriend and her man. Lots of laughter, getting-to-know-you stories, smiles. All through the meal and conversation, Bob can't let go of Andrea's forearm. He holds and strokes it the entire evening. When everyone has left and the dishes are done, Bob and Andrea talk and... fall asleep in each other's arms.

Saturday, July 28th, 2007: In the morning, Bob thinks, "Love over sixty...hmmmm. Who knew it would be better than love at any other age?" The first love poems are already taking form within him. But right now, he has business to take care of-- a client coming in for a leadership retreat. He must return home. It is painful to separate so quickly, but they are grownups. They can do this.

From that moment forward, Bob and Andrea spend every possible minute together.

Thursday, August 2nd, 2007: Bob returns to Andrea's cottage. He can conduct most of his business from anywhere since it is by phone and email. On his fourth day back, he holds her close and says words he never thought he'd say again...and definitely hasn't planned. "I don't know if this matters to you, but I want you to be my wife some day."

Andrea looks into his eyes and says, "I want to be your wife."

There are no "we must be crazy...this is moving too fast...this is too good to be true...we're acting like a couple of kids" thoughts in their heads. Well, actually, yes on the "we're acting like a couple of kids," but only in a joyful, positive way. They adopt two mottos. First is "a deep simple life." That's what they want to create together—a life of depth, not speed. Second is, *"no green bananas."* They've both been alive too long and have suffered too many sudden losses to believe they have a guarantee of time. Others may fret that they're rushing it. Bob and Andrea are too busy creating a whole new universe to pay attention to those cautions.

Andrea has told Leonard about Bob. In his own way, he has indicated his blessing. He wants Andrea to be happy. Bob meets Leonard on this return visit. Leonard is content watching TV in his little room. He makes eye contact with Bob and manages to shake hands with his left hand, the right one being curled up from the stroke like a knot of wood. Leonard offers a few words and phrases such as "wonderful, wonderful" and "thank you very much." When Bob notices he is watching an old black and white movie with Jimmy Stewart, Leonard is able to hit the right button on the remote to call up the linear key showing the movie's title, year and its stars. He begins to point to the words on the screen and struggle to say something else. Bob and Andrea wait patiently but in spite of his gestures and their guessing, the connection isn't made.

"It's often like this," Andrea tells Bob. "Some of his long term memory is still good…so he can recall things about these movies and the actors and even where he was when he first saw them…but he just can't get the words. The part of his brain that produces speech is pretty much gone. So this is it. This is about all he can say."

It's heart-gripping for Bob to see this man who was a brilliant architect reduced to such limited self-expression and experience. What a strange irony that his stroke is what has made this glorious new love possible.

Mid to late August, 2007: Andrea had committed months before to a trip to Costa Rica with her daughter and granddaughter. She is gone for two weeks. Poems and words of passion are zip-lining back and forth through satellite signals and phone lines until Andrea returns… with phone charges nearly equal to the annual national budget of Costa Rica.

Bob says, "This is the kind of thing teenagers would do…and stick their parents with the bill."

Andrea answers, "Yes, but we are the parents!"

Bob thinks, "Love over sixty…just like love at sixteen, only we get to pay the bills!"

September to Mid-October, 2007: They continue to spend most of their time together at Andrea's cottage. However, she does visit Bob's home on the Central Coast of California a few times and is reminded of what a magnificent area it is. Each of them has a sense of urgency, knowing they don't have forty, fifty or sixty years ahead of them. They will soon acknowledge that within a day of their face-to-face meeting, they were both quietly thinking about moving so they could make a life. They know long distance relationships are difficult or doomed if the couple doesn't find a way to be together in a timely manner. Bob has been thinking through how he would do his business from Andrea's town, how he would visit his son.

Andrea looks around at Bob's realm on her second visit and says,

"What a wonderful place! I'll move here. I've wanted to get out of Southern California for a while now." Bob is thrilled but not surprised. He has quickly learned that his new love is an adventurous and decisive person.

In mid-October, they are cruising around San Luis Obispo, getting a feel for the real estate and neighborhoods. They have a three-day convention to go to so they're not planning to examine any properties. However, Andrea sees a couple of well-dressed women taking photographs of a house and asks Bob to pull over. "Are you the agents?" she asks.

"Yes, we are…what are you looking for?"

Andrea quickly explains that they'd be interested in a house with an apartment out back where Leonard could live.

"You know, I think I might have just the ticket for you," says one of the agents. "Would you like to follow me across town?"

Five minutes later, Andrea and Bob pull up in front of a steep-roofed home they can't quite place architecturally—maybe French, maybe storybook Tudor—but it is definitely charming. They look at each other and almost simultaneously say, "Uh-oh, we're in trouble!"

The house is about eighty years old. Out back, there is a charming carriage house, perfect for Leonard. They'll have to make some changes for him, mainly by enlarging and handicapping the bathroom, but it's workable.

Twenty-four hours later, they make an offer. They have known each other two and a-half months.

Mid-October through November, 2007: More loving, poetry, working and negotiating over the house. They head to an ocean front condo in Costa Rica for two weeks over Thanksgiving. They walk the beaches, go zip-lining in mountain rainforests, explore the jungle for birds, butterflies, emerald snakes, tarantulas, cutter ants and tree-hanging sloths. Andrea manages to get a turkey and throws together a magnificent Thanksgiving dinner for just the two of them. Still more loving, poetry, reading and negotiating over the house back in the States. They close the deal by email before returning home.

December 20, 2007: Escrow closes on the house. Bob moves from his home about 10 miles south of town. Andrea, Leonard and Sofie the silver wonder-husky arrive the next day to spend the holidays in the new digs. It is five months to the day since their first emails and phone chats. *No green bananas! Not even one!*

February 5, 2008: The moving van arrives and Andrea, Leonard and Sofie move permanently into the new house with Bob.

February 5-May 31, 2008: Andrea and Bob strip, pound, sand, shave and paint their new house into a home. Andrea is particularly adept around the house—more of a handyperson than Bob in his wildest dreams, which is fine with him. He's busy celebrating her in poetry… although he does invest four days with her stripping their eighty-year old front door of roughly ten layers of paint.

Leonard settles in nicely. The new cottage is about twice the size of the room he had down south. A handicap bathroom is installed. He has his big flat-screen TV and he has Ida Lupino, Oliva de Havilland, Ray Milland, Fred and Ginger, Gene Kelly, Edward G. Robinson and all the other great stars he loved growing up. In mid-April, their friend David arrives from England. David is a licensed caregiver back home and loves caring for Leonard while having a place to stay in the States. He moves into one of the downstairs bedrooms and relieves Andrea and Bob of the daily chores of tending to Leonard. They are free to enjoy spending leisure time with him, taking him to movies, going for rides with him to enjoy the architecture of the area and its physical beauty.

On May 2nd, they head for Peru, realizing Bob's long-held dream. Arriving in the Sacred Valley of the Incas at ten thousand feet, Andrea is immediately taken by the magic. "I had no idea it would be so beautiful! Let's buy property!" This idea will be a regular part of their conversations and a running joke as they explore the land of the Incas. The magic calls from everywhere. Unlike most tourists who spend only a day at Machu Picchu, they stay nearly a week. One morning, they discover a young silversmith in the town below the ruins. They're looking for a matching ring set and find one within a few minutes. It might as well have been custom made for them. The rings are silver with three bands of lapis in each. They fit perfectly and cost the tidy sum of $24! The next day, Andrea and Bob make the two-hour hike to the Temple of the Moon around the back of Huayna Picchu.

When they arrive, the cave Bob had imagined for their vows is occupied by a half-dozen people. He leads Andrea around the corner where they sit in solitude on a stone terrace built by Inca masons.

Their vows flow from them. They know they are the receivers of a great blessing. They know how fragile it can be. They know they *don't* know how much time they have left on this planet. It might be tempting to see it as near tragedy that they found each other so late in life, but they will not succumb to these thoughts. They promise to stay deep in each other's eyes. to be real, open and honest, to love each other fiercely to the end. They promise that if either one of them drifts away from the center of their love, the other will go out and bring him or her back. They share the dream to live long, to stay healthy and to ultimately die in each other's arms.

All this they share quietly, surrounded by jungle and Inca stones. They kiss, laugh and wonder out loud if those who set these stones on which they are sitting ever imagined hundreds of years ago that two people would come here one day from a faraway land to consecrate their love. It is May 14th, 2008—nine months and seventeen days since they met.

June-September 2008: Andrea and Bob spend a lot more time stripping, pounding, painting, tiling, fencing, planting, going to the movies, reading and talking about combining their professional skills together in some way.

Halloween, 2008: Andrea and Bob are legally married in the States, on a cliff by the sea, surrounded by a few family members, at least a thousand pelicans and a smell nobody will forget!

March, 2009: While Andrea is still taking a sabbatical before starting up a practice in her new town, Bob has continued to work as a consultant. The economy has certainly trimmed back his load so he decides it's a good time to broaden his education. He hadn't anticipated going back to school at age sixty-two, but what the heck. He has a good reason. He can become certified to assist Andrea in her work as a Licensed Marriage and Family Therapist so they can realize their dream of working together. She is an advanced clinician in Imago Relationship Therapy, the couples work developed by Dr. Harville Hendrix, author of *Getting the Love You Want*. She has been practicing this model for more than sixteen years and has found it to be by far the most effective way to help couples work through conflict constructively, deepen their intimacy and grow together. Bob has read Hendrix's book and found it largely congruent with his personal and professional experience. Andrea has introduced some of the practices into their relationship. They make real every day sense to Bob. He sees how they slow two people down, create safety and nurture exchanges that are true and beautiful, turning potentially difficult moments into authentic growth. He jumps in with both feet. Andrea audits all the seminars to support Bob. Soon, they both enroll in the training to deliver the two-day *Getting the Love You Want Couples Workshop* Dr. Hendrix has designed to introduce couples to Imago. Andrea has never been interested in doing this in the past. She has been content to work with one couple at a time. But now, in Bob she has a real partner with complementary skills.

May, 2009: Andrea and Bob find a perfect loft for their new undertaking in the heart of downtown. The San Luis Relationship Institute is about to be born. Is this the deep simple life they had talked of? Probably not simple, but definitely deep. Anyway, the economy isn't making simple as accessible as it seemed just two years earlier. Like a lot of baby boomers, they now see themselves working many more years, as long as they have the vitality to make a contribution and the trade-off of time for money is sensible.

July-August, 2009: Approaching their second anniversary together, they finish decorating and furnishing the Institute, preparing to open it officially in the fall. They continue their education with the Imago Therapy community, relax in the evenings watching entire seasons of their favorite TV shows, hike, bike, eat healthy food, walk the local beaches with Sofie, take care of Leonard and laugh about green bananas!

Fall, 2009: Bob receives certification as an Imago Educator. He and Andrea officially open the San Luis Relationship Institute.

Bob realizes he has written well over forty love poems for Andrea. It strikes him they might just make a book…

To learn more, visit: www.loveover60.com and www.slrii.com .

Poems

The Choice
for Annie

Love chose us
    long before we met,
so long
    no one but Love herself
could know,
    quietly encouraging
        nudging
    sometimes kicking us
…closer and closer,
    even when we seemed
further and further
    from her handy
        …or foot work;
although,
    there were times
        across decades
I sensed you were coming,
    felt you in the next room,
        around a corner
        across the street,
…the intimation of your presence
    in the presence of a lesser love.
        I could smell you,
        almost make out
            your eyes
        the lines of your lips
    the way you'd ask a question,
        disagree,
come through a door with a bag of groceries,
        sit,
            sip tea;
I almost knew exactly what would anger
    or inspire you,
how certain words

        would engage your teeth and tongue,
how consciousness would move forward
    from the backs of your eyes,
how you'd shape
    childhood stories,
        share troublesome dreams,
        whisper endearments.
At times
    it was so strong
    I could almost draw your outline
        in the air
    ...almost,
        but then,
            you were gone.

We thought we could
    control Love,
        tell her how to
            paint and sing.
We wanted only
    pretty pictures
        and sweet songs.
Our ideas of perfection
    were not the same as Love's.
Love was so much smarter.
    She carefully prepared
    our way
    luring us through miseries
    we did not seek or understand.
Who would ask for suffering
    without a guarantee of redemption
        --the women with
    dark-throated songs
        who clawed at my ventricles,
the men who made you pay for
    their sweetness with savagery
        ...who would choose such a fate,

    confirm in the thick of it
        that the thick of it
was necessary,
    and in its own way,
        good?

But Love knows her craft.
She has made of us a
        a picture
    of her own perfection
   with subtle shadings
we could never have managed.
All the dangerous steps
    we've walked
        hold their places
          like
shadows and blood
    in the background
        of a painting
        celebrating the end of war.

Love chose us. She most certainly did.
We had nothing to do with that mystery,
     only the obligation to stagger forward
     believing and disbelieving
until this moment…
    this moment
when we finally know her will.
    Even so
it feels necessary
       to choose
with active arms
    what she has chosen for us.
So here I affirm, for my own part,
    sweet woman,
I choose Love's work.
    I choose you

        and only you,
your voice and mouth
your eyes and skin
    your fingers and fingertips
    the nape of *your* neck
    the back of *your* knee
    the flesh of *your* forearm
        and no other's,
your nightmare
your daybreak
your grief and glory
        and no other's,
your wildness
    and willfulness
your shadows and blood
    and no other's,
        absolutely no other's
            ever.
I choose Love's
    incomprehensible
        perfection
    manifest
        in you,
    only
you.

The Cradle Won't Fall
for Annie

So I had entered my sixty-first year,
thinking,
"I really want one more chance at love...
    one more chance
    to have my world rocked
    and rock someone's in return."
One moment, it seemed possible,
the next
    a pipe dream.

But
  here
    it
      is.
You and I
definitely rocking each other's worlds.
We'd both clung to the idea
    we were living in full sun before.
        Yet now
    plants leap from our soil
        clapping their leaves.
    Birds sing themselves silly
        and fall from their perches.
    Dogs start barking
      or stop
    for reasons they can't understand.
They chase their tails and catch them
        befuddled as to what to do next.
The lion and the lamb are consorting,
    the giraffe and hyena,
    the hippo and hedge hog,
though God only knows what they have to talk about.
But then,
    that's the whole point, isn't it?

The impossible and the ridiculous
become real in this love.
Speaking of impossible and ridiculous,
    in our world
there *is* peace on earth good will towards men,
well, at least towards this man and this woman
...the rest of the world, by and large,
    having foresworn
        or dismissed such sentiments
           as
    greeting card aspirations.

The neighbor's cats
    are in the window
        doing as cats do
    licking each other's faces
which only reminds me how much wiser they are
        than most humans,
    present company excepted,
        since we know very well what
to do with our tongues
    sitting up here
        closer to the top of life's tree
than either of us has ever been,
    grooming and holding each other
                  cradle-close
    where the wind may indeed rock us
    but the bough
    will not break.
We defy that old nursery rhyme.
We'll be children together
    climbing, swinging and singing
        all the way to the very top branch
           till we step off into heaven.

Bright Form
for Annie

"The word of god shines bright in the form of man."
   --Hildegarde von Bingen

Before you and I
became *us*
the word was not
    shining
anywhere
day or night.
It was merely there,
acceptable
but not notable
    and certainly not bright.
The moon had never been full,
    merely a thin tear
        in the sky
            through which
                a small smile
                leaked
    …and starlight
ran down
    night's walls,
        graffiti in the rain.

We each knew we'd survive
    even enjoy life
but knew as well
    that enjoy is not *in* joy;
sometimes,
    cynicism's tide rose so high
we thought
    there might
        finally be
an end to metaphors.
Everything would simply be what it was,

no less,
    but certainly no more,
and the idea that love could renew
      our senses
with endless inventions
      of tongue, tone
      and phrases
was fast becoming
    quaint on its way
    to dumb.
Life would always be incomplete
because love would always be incomplete.

Then came
    this moment—the stone steps
        five strides
            through your garden
and shining in the doorway,
    you
and everywhere
    bright openings.
Time-bound imperfections
      exited our memories.
In their absence,
      we forgot
          to doubt.

That night
    the moon
        threw off
            its shawl of shadows
                and sang
        full force
        in a new language
we were
    the first
to hear.

Crazy Beautiful
for Annie

All right.
You believe in past lives
    and I don't
at least, not yet.
    But it has never been so easy for me
to allow that difference.
I must admit to wondering, though…
    how does it happen
that in our first email
you ask if I've read a book
    so few on the planet have read
and I say, "Yes, and loved it"?
And a little while later,
I ask if you've read another book
    so few have read
and you say,
"Yes, that's one of my favorite books on love."
How does this happen?
And then you say,
"Yeah, I've tended to be a rescuer in my life,"
and I say,
"Me, too, probably my biggest weakness
    in relationships"
and you say,
"Yeah, hard lesson to own,"
and I say,
"Yeah, but we got there,"
and you say,
"We did, didn't we?"
How does it happen
    that we're both
        psychological and artistic,
eminently overqualified, you might say,
    to understand each other…??

How does it happen that we both love
    amber and architecture,
        Latin American countries
    with big flowers
      big fruit
        and big jungles?
How does it happen
    that you know a pig named, Lola,
and the only pig I've ever known
    was named Lola.
(Is "Lola" like "Mary" for pigs?)
How does it happen
    you have a husky dog
and I always wanted one
    (even drew its face when I was seven)
and her name is Sofie
    and that's one of my favorite names…??
How does it happen
    that you figure out "who done it"
      in the first five minutes of all the cop shows
        before there's even a crime,
      just like my mother did?
And how does it happen
that we fall in love on the phone
    and then the first time
we see each other
        slide
    into a kiss that lasts an hour
…and then, when we come up for air,
you give me a card that says,
    "I thought I'd never find you"
and, after forty years of being an adult,
    that's exactly what I'm thinking?
And we both love
    simple food—vegetarian—and dark chocolate
    and figs with honey and blue cheese on them,
      kalamata olives and almonds…

and we're both adventurous-expressives
    so out front with who we are
    that some people run away screaming!
How does it happen
    that we can make love with such
        honesty and surrender
from the very first time
and at an age when many people aren't getting naked
at all anymore, except in front of their doctors?
How does it happen
    we love the same movies
    and kinds of people
    and furniture and chatchkes
from foreign lands,
    but above all
    each other…hmmm?
And tell me, especially,
    how does it happen that years ago
        on one side of the country
a Tarot lady told me
    I'd become The Magician
        and another Tarot lady
on the other side of the country said
you'd become The Queen of Pentacles
…and decades later
    another lady
—a silly gorgeous soul—
who already knew you,
    met me
and decided right away we should be together
and tried for eight years to make it so
and then
    finally
        actually
            pulled it off!
I mean, what are the odds here??
    Is there a genius bookie in the house?

Maybe you're right.
    Maybe we have
    been together
        in past lives...
maybe two bees on the same flower
    or prisoners in the same tower
    or betrothed beneath the same bower
    or chimes of a church bell at the very same hour
...or maybe,
in some way we're not meant to understand,
we conjured each other
    out of the field of all possibilities
    and it's just
crazy beautiful, beyond explanation...
    or
        maybe
    both
because the universe is the real Magician,
    the real Queen of Pentacles.
With so many
    quantum percolations going on,
        past lives
        and
        crazy beautiful
          are bound to happen
            to someone sooner or later.
Well, my darling lady,
it looks like they did.
    They happened to us.
And maybe the very least
    even a confirmed cynic can say is
    that with all the dust and detritus
        the universe has churned out,
it did, in fact, have a very good day
    when it managed
to lasso us from such
    distance

   and tie us
      together in
     this big
        strong
           gentle
              knot.

Sixty-Sex
for Annie

So a younger
    fortyish friend
was audacious enough to ask me today,
    "Is there sex after sixty?"
I thought,
    "OH
        MY
            GOD!
Sixty-Sex!
Let's-get-naked-right-this-second sex;
kundalini-unleashing ,
chakra-shaking,
furniture-breaking sex,
spine-and-mind-bending,
can't-get-enough-of-every-inch-of-you,
hopelessly-romantic sex,
we'll-have-to-invent-an-entirely-new- language
    -to-describe-it sex,
hey-diddle-diddle-
the-cat-and-the-fiddle-
way-out-over-the-moon sex,
beauty-and-beast,
spirit-in-body,
    I love you
        I love you
            I love you
                sex,
    sixty-sex!"

I thought all that,
    my darling,
        but
    didn't
        say
            a word.

The Unmeasure of Love
for Annie

There are no adjectives adequate for love,
no metaphors whose mime can measure up.
We try, though,
    tossing words
    as if spraying paint at sunlight
hoping a form will emerge
    to define it for us.
  But love
      is a wave
not a particle
    and not a single wave
        but an ocean of them
moving
    in every possible direction
        at once
            --a happy delirium
whose dimensions
    and intentions
        make perfect sense
    the instant
        our bodies
            touch.

Divine Breath
for Annie

The gods whisper through us,
    use us
        as instruments
to awaken the world.
Their breath
    is wind
moving low across the river
wearing sunlight
    on its back.

The gods speak through us
    use us
        as instruments
to teach the world.
Their breath
    is wind
rising from the caves
    where our fathers sleep,
wind wearing darkness
    on its back.

The gods sing through us
    use us
        as instruments
to move the world.
Their breath
    is wind
plunging from the summits
unfurling
    a cape
        of stars.

Sweet Phrasing
for Annie

I am your other
    and you are mine.
And this indisputably makes us
  "each other's other"
    -an awkward phrase,
      perhaps, even bitter
        …in someone else's mouth
but not in yours
  and not in mine.
    …more like peach juice
      just as it releases
between the teeth.

Behind the Dream
for Annie

    Hidden
by a dream
    for years,
the real you
    emerged
        as much more
    mysterious
alluring
    and precise
than that
    seductive
        shimmer
…the dream of flesh
    no match for yours,
the dream of lips,
    eyes, hair, voice
        no match for yours
but even less
    a match for how
    your complex heart
paved a path to mine
    and walked right in,
        nakedness
          inviting
            nakedness,
      far more exact
    far softer
        than the dream.

New Mosaic
for Annie

That was the night
        we came so close
    we were thrown apart
filtered through
galaxies of sunflowers
    into the finest
        powder
—grist for a new mosaic
on the other side of the universe,
    a new planet
        of blue canyons,
        high suns,
        endless fields of flowers
        that bloom long and sing
            when their petals fall...
and a new tree of life that stands on a bluff
    roots wound in rock,
    limbs wound in sky
    ...where every lake looks like an eye
    and every eye a lake
--a place the great explorers fear more
    than serpents, dragons and so-called savages,
    a place where heartbeats are heard
        from over the next rise
            so quiet is the air.

Beast on Beast
for Annie

It's worth noting
    I think
that when it came time to remove
the last household items from
    the POD
whose alien being
    had occupied our driveway
    for three months,
its ribbed guts stuffed
    with enough belongings
to fully furnish a second home…
it's worth noting
    I think
that when it came time
    for the very last items
to be disgorged,
you
    were away,
        which was good,
yet not so good…
because you were not here
to see your sixty year-old lover
take on your elliptical exerciser
which had steadfastly held
    its intimidating pose
in the very depths of the POD's belly
--a prehistoric creature
of some two hundred plus pounds
    on the verge of evolving arms to wings.
Your old man
    unleashed his inner Neanderthal
with all its squat fury
    to slide, twist, grunt,
    curse and scream

this beast
    from the belly of the POD
emerging into sunlight
    with a sense of triumph
and certainty
that the story would wind around
many a campfire
    for many a generation
…most cogently,
that this sixty year-old man, your lover,
    accomplished this terrible task
without popping
    a single pill
or any cherished muscle
…bullied and chastised
    the beast a good thirty feet
into the backyard
    where it cowered under the carport
and finally purred
    in submission to my awful Alpha-ness.
It's worth noting
    I think
and good you weren't there to worry over me
for I enjoyed the contest
    though its end was tinged with sadness
as I thought
    "She will never see the twenty year-old me,
    torso tight as a tree
as I wrestled down
    far bigger foes
    without giving a first
    no less a second
        thought
to hernias."

Pretty Good Eaters
for Annie

We are pretty good eaters
you 'n I.
We eat the fruits and veggies
    cause we want to live.
We eat the wild salmon
    cause we want to live.
We eat the whole grains
the raw nuts
and lots and lots and lots of broccoli,
shitake mushrooms
and the crunchy celery
and the asparagus and spinach.
We eat these things
    cause we want to live
and live upright
without titanium joints,
ambulatory and spry
dancing on the twinkles
in each other's eyes
slurping the smoothie
and spooning up the yogurt
and munching down the goji berry
and snapping
and cracking the dark chocolate
    cause we want to live
and live long.
Having found each other late
we are greedy
truly greedy,
greedy
to keep going
and going strong
beating back the ravages,
savages and averages

    of age
and holding high the laughter
with our leaping hearts.
We want to live.
    We want to live
        because
            because
                because
                    we love!!

Force of Nature
for Annie

The rain
    your breathing
…can't tell them apart,
    but the lightning,
that was clearly
    you.

Complements
for Annie

I am hunting
    for a word
the
    word
        to place just so
and cast color
    into a white space
so the mind of another
    will be taken
        somewhere
it hasn't been
    recently
or ever
on the outside edge of describable.
    Joyous!

You are hunting for a color
    the
        color
to cast across a wall
    in a particular room
    so the mind of another
will be taken
    somewhere
it hasn't been
    recently
or ever
    just inside the border of ineffable.
        Joyous!

I wander
    the interior bazaar
in and out of stalls and shops
    bartering and bantering

with the congress of my soul
--scoundrels and singers,
    villains and saviors--
feeling my way through spoken textures,
    patterns, blends, aromas
my hand may render
    into keyboard taps
        or trails of ink.

You wander the exterior
    bazaar
in and out of stalls and shops
        bartering and bantering
    with the congress of vendors
a cacaphony of many-feathered birds
        wrapped in the smell
of incense and sweat
    --wheelers and pitchmen
    deceivers and true believers—
feeling your way through fabrics,
    fixtures,
        ornaments
            and oddities
so your hands
    may render
the reality of a house
    into a home.

We are hunters and handlers,
    you and I,
till the poem or room
    is crafted
from an energy
    well beyond the work of tongues
    --a place
        where
we have plunged our arms

  shoulder deep
   in eternity's waters
and pulled up something
   true and beautiful,
something we sensed
  might
    be graspable
  if only
our breaths and hearts
  were adequately
love-driven,
  love-laden,
    love-bound.

The Chair
for Annie

Of course you remember
    that evening
I invited you into my office
to look at images of Peru.
You asked if it was okay
to bring in the antique chair
with the small weaving tied to its seat,
a very light chair
of which my mother
knew quite a bit
and I know next to nothing
except that I like its curves and openness
(though not as much as I like
your curves and openness).
The weaving never caught my eye before
but now that you're gone
and the chair is here
I find myself moving the whole of my palm
back and forth across it and remembering
the texture of your skin
which is far more like buttermilk
than silk or wool;
And I find myself feeling a painful
    appreciation
of the weaving's colors,
    colors I never really noticed before,
beige, dark brown, blue, pink and blood red
arranged in very specific patterns
that must mean something
in the weaver's culture,
    a culture of which I am wholly ignorant
except for its obvious holiness.
It probably has something to do with
birth, love and death

      something to do with quenching
     what seems an endless longing
        in the heart of man,
something to do with the search
    for a certainty of godliness hiding
      in all this darkness
         like a hundred candles
      waiting to be lit.

But that takes the theme too far
    for me
right now.
Right now
    at this moment,
there seems to me a small
but certain holiness
    in leaving this chair
right where you left it
    till you return
and strike a match
to the one big candle
    waiting
on the darkened
      hillside
    of my heart.

Our Island
for Annie

He wakes up
    far too early,
        around three AM,
starts to get up
but she says,
    "No, honey, stay in bed."
He rolls back onto his pillow.
She spoons against him.
He says,
    "My brain is going far too fast
    for a man of six decades"
She says,
    "I know…but think of an island.
Just think of an island
Just the two of us
and beautiful calm blue waves
and orchids everywhere."
He says,
    "Okay, I'll try…hmmm, an island
    just for the two of us…
    a secret senior get-away
        …with no mosquitoes?"
"Of course not,"
she says, "It's our island
We can make it as we wish."
He says,
    "And no poisonous snakes
    or scorpions
    or ticks or fleas
        or predatory bees,
no coconuts except those that drop
right into our hands…"
She says,
    "It's our island.
We can make it as we wish."

She squeezes him.
He's got it now.
    "No plunging Dow
    or real estate values,
no rising unemployment
    or global temperatures,
no talking heads,
no infomercials,
no, not
even
sunburn!
It's our island.
We can make it as we wish.
No wild boars,
just friendly pot-belly pigs
No schistosomiasis."
    "Hey," she says,
"you're getting carried away, now!"
    "None of that either," he says.
    "No getting carried away,
especially by fire ants, cannibals or crocodiles.
It's our island.
Our island," he says,
"We can make it as we wish
…and no one else sets foot
unless we invite them."
"Yes," she says,
"unless we invite them.
    Sound good?"
He lets out a long tropical sigh
and whispers,
    "I can't answer now.
    I'm asleep on our beach
under our palm tree
…with the highly considerate coconuts.
    G'night my love."
"Good night, Island Man."

Callings
for Annie

I didn't come
    empty
into this world.
    My pockets
        were chocked
with words and images,
    that made perfect sense
        in a place
of earlier origins
    but nearly none in this.
The exact source
    is still unknown to me
        ….something to do, perhaps,
            with lost footprints
        on an African plain,
a creature with its own
    unique music,
        burbled and wailed
        from a mind
    awakening
to the implications
    of its new uprightness;
    or more distant…
a place before
    a whiff of humanity
        hit the wind;
a tiny intelligence within the shell of a cell,
    more compact and potent
        than my own today
    able to record
on the micro-pages of its mitochondria
    blades of grass
        gasping through
            dried lake bottoms,

the low gutturals of lizards,
    the melodies of moonlight.

Still, I was called to reconfigure
the fragments
brought in from those times and places,
    to shape images with sounds,
sounds with images,
    tuck small scrolls
        here and there
    in knotholes
        and outcroppings
    along the way
  from my first uncertain stand
    far forward to a future
where my legs no longer lift themselves
    to clear a river rock.
For what purpose
    this travail
mating the invisible with the visible,
if not to say in my own way,
    "I was here and beheld the beauty".

This calling brought me to a second
    --fatherhood;
not just its responsibility,
  but its lyric essence
    which I was drawn to
        by my son himself,
    a tiny intelligence
more compact and potent than my own,
    a tenderness
        hilarity
            and joy
                big as sunrise;
called to catch from his spray of
                      lights

    sounds and images
        enough
          to stain pages
    and score the air with song;
        this calling
    served by the first
a purposeful travail
    to say in my own way,
"I was here and beheld his beauty."

And now
    the third time called
        ...to you, my darling,
    and to us
    --a most unexpected clarion
six decades on;
    a new and necessary forgetting
and re-entering this world,
    carrying with me
        the gorgeous echoes
    of an unintelligible ancient
        tongue;
you, across the river
    under a tree
        big as the sky itself,
entering the water
at the same moment as I,
    bringing yet more sounds
        unknown to me
            forms
        unknown to me
yet all shiveringly familiar
    as dream fragments recalled
in late afternoon.
In the middle
    I will reach you,
        hold you,

listen to the mystery
    you've carried all these years,
        study the rivers in your eyes
and the branches overhead
    and the roots beneath us,
reach back again
    to the time and place
    when love first left
its markings on the earth,
    retrieve an echo or a sign
        to
tuck inside these verses
    and fling them over the moon.
    For what purpose, this travail,
        if not, in the end,
        to say in my own way,
"I was here and beheld your beauty."

Unbounded
for Annie

We climbed up
    to the mountain of love
        you and I
to the summit of the mountain of love
to the top of the tree
    that grows there
on the summit of the mountain of love
    and there we became mythic children
    befrienders of sky
    counselors to clouds
    supplicants of sun, moon, wind
        and the
            deep
                bright
                    stillness
                        of love.

We went down
    through the creviced canopies
        into the jungle of love
where we spoke with the golden frog,
    the emerald snake,
    and the blue butterfly.
We hunted with fox and jaguar,
    laughed with coatimundi,
        howled
        with the monkeys and macaws
            in the thick-woven
                branches of love
        shimmied
        down
    the teak and tamarindo,
        the guanacaste,
        balsa

        and banyan
           into the orchid of love
    --the blood-throated chamber of love
        that held us
           in the darkness of love
      the deepness of love
        ...emerging to twine
                in the vine of love.

I am your life and your death
        your sanctuary,
        your sadness,
        your solace,
        your celebration
        and
    you are mine.

Out in the desert of love
        miles from the oasis of love
    we dared offer our doubts
        to the unnourished
            sands of love
        left them to die
    with appreciation
for the limited loves that led us to each other
    but could not reach or teach us any longer...
walked away
    hand in hand
        step in step
            heart in heart
    over the scalding dunes of love
        through the whirlwind of love
out to the big waters
    and down
        to the undersea forests of love

   the gaping canyons of love
   the submerged cemeteries
      and citadels of love
    covered by blankets
     of diatoms
      where the sleep is soft
      yet deep as death
  and waking
strong as birth
   the birth of mythical children
   befriending the sky
and all that is in it, below and above it
    in the sanctuary of love
   the sadness,
    the solace
      the celebration
      the bright
        stillness of love,
          this particular love,
unequaled, unbounded. Love

The Temple
for Anne

We walked a long way
    to make that promise
after waiting at the gate for our turn
to leave Machu Picchu
    on the Inca stairway
up and down
up and down
    down
        down
across the faces of huge green waves
      of jungle overhead
      and underneath
    one after the other,
      the humidity thick enough
        to stuff in a pocket
…a good two hours' walk
emerging into open space
    with real sky
      at the Temple of the Moon
only to find four or five people
    in the cave we had chosen
in advance as *our* place,
    each of them
      making furniture of the sculpted rocks,
        their eyes oblivious to the present
as they journeyed up and down
    up and down , down, down
      through the rising and falling of Inca
    transformations and tragedies
--inconvenient for us
    but also inconsequential
      for we were nimble and innovative!
We moved easily
beyond the cave

      to a side terrace
          just the right height
for comfortable sitting.
There we
    took each other's hands
    took each other's eyes
    took each other's hearts and souls
and promised
    to love each other to the very end
however that might manifest
(and we knew full well
    we could not know,
that it might be graceful
    but also might
well involve wheel chairs
    or far worse)
--a vow more real to us now
than any we might have made
    in our twenties or thirties
before we could feel in our viscera
    the full heft of the phrase
        "till death do us part".
I promised
    that if you lose yourself
and wander from
    the real space
    and real sky
        at the center of our love
I will go
    no matter how far,
        no matter how dangerous
    or confusing,
I will go out
    and find you
        …bring you back
           to be with me here
    in the fullness of our conscious love.

You promised the same
--for we are old enough to know this can happen.
   No matter how magnetic,
      humans come with compasses
         whose needles spin
           wildly
              from time to time;
everyone takes a mean
  or twisted turn
  now and then;
everyone gets lost
         …and we are no different.
But we vowed
  our wanderings
    would be brief
and the healing and wisdom would come
  fast
     and stay long.
We slipped on our silver and lapis rings
acquired that very day
  from a Quechua smith of considerable gifts.
We kissed and laughed and
  celebrated our head-on, heart-on collision
and knew ourselves to be the original platonic unity
  divided
    reunited,
opposite gender embodiments
  of the same soul
and certainly more firmly married
than if we'd had a formal wedding
  in the Vatican itself
  or the Supreme Court
or where the Temple of Solomon
  once stood in Jerusalem.
We were on holy ground right here.
The Quechuas made it holy.
We affirmed its holiness

and delighted, wondering out loud
if the builders of this particular terrace
    in their workday chatter
imagined that at some distant point in the future
two such as us
from a faraway land
    would make the long walk to pledge their hearts
    on this very spot
    where they placed these particular stones
with such care.
Love at any age is holy
    but all the more
        when two people
stand atop a hundred twenty years together
        and know quite well
what belongs to Incas and Caesars
    and what to God.
Today, this moment
even among their ruins
there is nothing left for Emperors.
These kisses are only God's
    these deep long kisses
--messages
    breathed through the tight necks
        of bottles
sealed and tossed across huge green waves
    to the far sides of our souls…
        these kisses
    that move each of us
    out of the sweltering thickets
onto pure beaches beneath huge skies
    where ours are the first and last footprints known
and voyaging bottles
and their lyric scrolls come to rest
    …pure beaches
    where the caress of a perfect breeze
        chases the heat from our bodies.

You are my perfect breeze
and I am yours.
You are my bottled message
    shaken free
        and I am yours.
The service of your heart
    shall be the purpose of mine
        here in the realm of
    water,
    leaf
    stone
    and moon.
Holy in our moment,
    we,
        holy in our love.

Wishes
for Annie

How could this love
    be more complete?
        Can a circle be rounder?

Okay, I admit
    from time to time
        I do wish
we'd been born
    side by side
on the same day
    in the same place
        at the same moment
...our mothers best friends
    our fathers best buddies.
Too much
    to wish
        no doubt
but love allows for high flying fantasies
    if only to describe its depths
        in ways that simple sentences
            cannot.
I also wish
    we'd spent hours side by side
        in the same crib
in a room with sun-yellow walls
    under the same slowly turning mobile
--clouds, stars, horses, fish—
and become aware of breezes in the room
        and music
at exactly the same second.
I do wish
    we'd bubbled from our lips
        our first consonants,
    crawling side by side toward

        a brightness
            beyond the doorway.

I could go on
    but don't need to
        knowing
            you feel
        what I feel
this moment
    so many years from our first.
Were these wishes true
    they might
make the circle larger
    but certainly
    not rounder
because
    our mouths do birth
        fresh consonants
            each day
                as we move
through sun-yellow rooms
                side by side
                    into
                      a
                    brightness
            beyond
                the doorway.

Shoes
for Annie

You,
the tidy house keeper
...a place for everything
    and everything in its place;
baskets, bins, boxes,
    dividers, hooks, hangars,
        upright and flat files
    labels and organizers,
        designated drawers,
mats and throw rugs at every entry
    towels wherever needed,
        everything in ample supply.
All done
    with your unique touch
--a color sense
painters and florists must envy,
    form to stimulate the salivary glands
of architects and sculptors,
    and function
the itchy fingers of dandruffed engineers.

But
    these shoes...
how to explain
    these shoes,
walked right out of
    in the middle of a doorway
or hallway
    even stairway
pumps, flip-flops, slippers, Uggs, sandals...
rebellious, insolent,
    even downright dangerous
and neglected,
    left for dead for days on end...

far too "in your face" to dismiss?

As young as five
    and probably younger
your mother put you on a stool
    to do dishes
--not a bad thing to ask of a child,
    a task here or there
easing mom's load,
    learning responsibility;
no, really not such a bad thing in itself
    even when your friend, Martha, was calling up to you
from the Chicago streets,
    "Come out and play!"
and the answer,
    on many an evening was, "No,
I have chores to do"
…until
your sisters and brother came along.
    To the dishes were added diapers
and housework
and herding the little tribe
    around the neighborhood
    safely
    happily
--a tall order many adults
couldn't manage.
    No wonder it was critical to
have a place for everything and
    everything in its place
lest a little brother be lost
    or sister be hurt
    and the blame
come crashing down
    on you.

So these shoes you leave

    here and there
in the midst of everything
    are, I think, a lasting message scrawled
        in the past
    declaring silently today,
        "But I'm a little girl!
I want someone to look after *me*,
    care for *me*,
        get things for *me*
            pick up
                after *me*!"

Well, my lady, you can leave your shoes wherever you like.
    I will look after you,
        care for you,
get things for you
    pick up after you.
And as I happily do so
I will hold a memory of you
    not from childhood
but a few months ago
    on the Inca pathway
    from Machu Picchu
down through the green gauze jungle
    to the Temple of the Moon
your hands held high
    beside your face
    for balance
and for joy.
    You stepped so lightly
    on the hard stone stairs
--a child
    leaping right out of her shoes
        into freedom.

Window Treatments, Cockroaches and Cat-Chicken
for Annie

In my dream
I'm wandering through a house
   --ours, presumably,
half renovated
   plywood
      sawdust
   nails scattered around
and these old vertical blinds
banging in the breeze of an open window
from which there's a view of the ocean
   and a dozen or more sailboats
      strung out in a straight line
half-way to the horizon
   like a beautiful sentence…
and the contractor asks me,
   "Whadya think?"
I say, "So far so good,
   but can we do something about
      the window treatments?"
I wake up laughing
   at how my feminine side has taken over
      since you cruised into my life,
my Annie-educated side, really,
   so much more sensitive to the fine touches
   --valences, blinds, pillows, candle-holders,
soap bottles, the presentation of hand-towels,
   coordinated colors
      that never knew such friendship
         till you introduced them!
   I always thought life was the ultimate art
but you've turned the noun to its most present verb.
Living is the ultimate art,
   the world we keep creating for ourselves every day
      down to the smallest detail.

And here comes your dream.
You're in Viet Nam preparing a meal for friends.
    You're given chicken, which you're sure is actually cat,
and juicy thumb-sized cockroaches.
You skewer the roaches, their legs still wriggling
    and wrap them in cat-chicken.
See…you couldn't just crisp the roaches.
    No.
You had to wrap them.
You can't let anything be ordinary,
    can you?
How terrible for me…
    putting up with
extraordinary
    marvelous
        outrageous
    exceptional
all-adjectives-on-deck *living*.
    Oh, really,
        how terrible for me!

Baggage and Truth
for Annie

They met in their sixties
so each of them had a heavy old chest
    of memories rolling behind
        on chattering wheels,
chests filled with carefully wrapped scarves
    hand-worked boxes
        artifacts of the early archaeology of love
    ...and false bottoms
where the deepest shames
    disguised themselves as wood on wood.
When questions arose
    about the women who came before
        he thought about whether or not to answer them
    fully.
Would the truth hurt her unnecessarily,
    make her doubt him?
Would she see it all as the path
    he had to walk to finally pass through her front door
        or
evidence of some pattern
    that might lead him out the back?
Should he shape and shave the truth
    as imperfectly explicable as it was
or trust that she could handle it unedited?

And surely, she
    contemplating her own past
    faced the same thicket of questions
though her romances were fewer
    and, she thought,
        easier to accept.
The simplest arithmetic may be the most difficult
    --truth plus zero equals truth--
but that's the calculation each made,

    each time
        quicker than a comma can be marked on a page.
There *were* tears
        and sometimes shame and blame,
lightning quick feints and parries,
    well-practiced
        in a past
where lovers became enemies
    without ever knowing why.
But now
    repeatedly they would find
their way beyond
    the strife
        back to the larger reality
(and faster each time
    precisely because they were no longer novices
and knew what was at stake)
    --a love far deeper and more real
    than any that had come before,
        the love
they had not only longed for,
    trained for,
    searched for,
    believed in
    when life gave them no reason to believe,
      …a love
        the inevitable child
            of destiny's long labor in them both,
        exquisitely innocent,
            even at this age,
            and the last
                either
                would ever need
                    or know.

An End to Ordinary
for Annie

I declare
    an end
to the ordinary
    old ways.
Writing on the air
    in smoke,
        on clay, papyrus, stone, wood,
            weavings.
    Even the poundings of new digital drums
are insufficient to tell the world of this love.
Wait while I
    arrange birds across the sky in verses,
        change the lines of sand dunes
            into metaphors of you,
    carve the trunks of every mighty tree
        so our names can ride the arrows,
etch the night with fire and the day with sharp shadows,
    tattoo the arms of the moon,
        confound the coordinates of time, place and cycle.
We are the new Theory of Everything.
    All is resolved.
            Physicists,
    rejoice!

Poems I'll Never Write for You
for Annie

There are poems
I'll never write for you.
I'm not into arbitrarily working the alphabet
    so you're not going to get a poem
        from me
    about an aardvark
        or a zygote
(although they might be worth mentioning in passing,
but passing what…I don't know—a kidney stone?).
I'm not likely to romance
    hamburger meat
        Brussels sprouts
            or shallots
                for you.
I will probably never turn my pen
    to render
        the small ballet
            you
                do
        mopping
            the hardwood floors.
I'm unlikely to write
    a mighty tidy rime
    about the mites
        that nearly slew
            the nephritis you bought.
I'm probably not going to rhapsodize
    your triumphs over soap scum.
But above all,
I'm highly unlikely to versify
    in detail
        about your many special talents
        on the playground
            of our bed.

They would be world-famous,
    if the paparazzi knew.
But
    I am sixty-two,
        not twenty or thirty-two.
Young folks can rap and write
    all funky,
        hip,
    blasphemous
        and bold.
    I'm glad to yield it to them.
Our generation has a different take,
    not prudish,
        just private.
Still, don't fret.
    I will speak to you
        specifically
            and often
        of my admiration
    as we act out naughty chapters
        on the sheets.
But that's where it will end, my love.
    In this day and age
        some things
            are better left
            uninked.

Fountains and Youth
for Annie

Juan Ponce de Leon
    tromped
        through the Florida swamps
in search of the Fountain of Youth.
What an assumption!
    There *is* a Fountain of Youth.
You drink from it,
    you live forever.
This apparently was considered sane at the time.
      And
forget about scaling the mountains
    to sip-test
        rocky springs.
This magical spout is located in a flatland,
    a swamp, no less,
mosquitoes
    and gators
        bonused in!

I can't help thinking
    Juan's own youth
was marked by too much of something
    and too little of something else
for him to risk so much
    so far from home,
craving an exit from the flesh's
      ultimate dilemma.
I guess we'll never know
    since we're not even sure who his parents were
no less what they did or did not do
    to and for him.
We do know
    however
        that he,

      like other well-known explorers
          of the time,
did not believe that
    "happiness lies
        right under your eyes
            back in your own backyard."
It took more than 400 years for that simple wisdom
    to flow from the fount of Al Jolson's lips.
Maybe Al was thinking of the bedraggled de Leon
    when he wrote,
"You'll see your castle in Spain, through your window pane
    back in your own backyard."
…his way of saying, "Hey, Ponce, baby,
did you have to project your fantasy
    so far away?
Did you even *consider*
    for a second
    the possibility that
love is the only
    real Fountain of Youth
and you needn't venture
    any further
than your own backyard
    or the backyard
        of the girl next door?"
Guess not!
    Would have been too easy
        for someone
            so lathered
                with grandiosity.
Being brutally single-minded
    may get you
        previously unknown continents,
        slaves,
        gold,
        chocolate
        and fountains of blood

>   in which to grow
>   the crops of the new world
> but it doesn't get you eternal youth.
> For that
> you need the wisdom of the obvious
> a wholly different kind of courage
> and a far shorter voyage
> ...like the one
>   I make each morning
> from my eyes
>   to
> the bright,
>   youthful
>   waters in yours.

A Saying of the Father
for Annie

Once I heard
   my father
      say,
"I sure love my boys,
   but
      they will grow up
   and leave
      some day,
as well they should…
but never
   will my wife."
Yes, my father spoke like that.
His journalistic gift was always present.
   And, further, he said,
" I hate to think of choosing,
   but sometimes it does come to that
--the economics of time and love—and
when it does,
      it's her, hands down."

When I was only the son
   these words
      punched the air
         from my lungs.
"How could I have a smaller space
   in his heart
      than hers?
Can't he see how very much I need to be first, too?"

Well, the economics of time and love
   walked them sixty-nine years
      hand-in-hand.
Now, I the motherless,
   fatherless

   son
  but also father
    of the son,
understand
  there really is an end
    to child-rearing.
Once my boy,
  now a man
    swings a scythe
      in his own field.
He has chosen
  a good place
not so far away
  but far enough.
His own son
  close by
    studies the
     fist and shoulder of his dad
even as the blackbirds come
  for their share of harvest now
—the supply and demand of life.

You and I,
  sweet love,
    together
stand
  and stay
    side by side,
      hands down
       holding
        each other's.
Our eyes study
  no far horizons
yet are happy
within the tiny temple of our nearness.

We know

            the black birds will scythe
                    through us soon
            till we've become
                    the harvest
            and the harvest song
    hummed by our children
                as they pause
    to catch
            their breaths
                    and wonder at
                            how fast
                                    a field is cut.

Sunlight and Shadows
for Annie

This is the tough stuff.
This is why most run.
Stronger the sunlight
    darker the shadow.
We thought we'd be immune.
"You are my warm wind,
    my water and my wine."
Foolish as youths
    …no one escapes.
"You are my bitter herb and my nectar.
I crave you and fear you,
    as you do me."
The homilies of pop psychology prove true.
We are a strange species
…temporarily, though frequently, insane.
The awesome power to hurt
--stronger the sunlight
    darker the shadow.
With God in each other's gaze,
    anything less feels like banishment.
Then,
I am not I
you not you
we not we.
The air is stolen
    by other voices
--mothers and fathers
      brothers and sisters
the early wounds writhing and whipping at each other
till blood is drawn and
    frozen rain hits the heart.
      We blink in darkness
        as strangers
wondering if we only dreamed the light.

No matter how old or wise we've grown,
    the unseen child cries to be seen,
    held,
        cherished for just being
on the bright side
of the Tree of Life
before prescribed behaviors turn to tyrannies
before heart is labeled sentimentalism,
a syndrome or disease or just bad taste
    to be scoffed at by politicians
        book reviewers
            art critics,
    even psychologists.

I know what it is to have Eden behind me
    and a frightful unknown before me.
I confess to angering the Creator.
I have felt his wrath on my back.
I confess to meanness.
I confess to behavior I would be ashamed for our children to see.
I confess to channeling the worst qualities of both my parents.
I confess to being unworthy of you.
Stronger the sunlight
    darker the shadow.

But we are not mere children.
We have lived.
We know things.
We know ways through and out.
I reach for your hand
and you for mine
We thought we were so far apart
    yet all along
were side by side
slumbering in the penumbra
    of this massive tree.

Love calls us to waken,
    to reach,
        to stand and take back
           our radiance
as we do now, this moment.
Darker the shadow,
    brighter the sunlight.

The Sweetness
for Annie

In the interest of full disclosure,
there are times when
    our lyricism seems lost.
        We misconnect
           or disconnect.
Sadly...or not,
this is part
of real love in a real world of
    hurt human beings.
Love is up to something
    quite different from what we expect
but (and I am so thankful for that conjunction)-
    the sweetness
        prevails,
          the sweetness I never imagined
...I, the fabricator of grandiose dreams,
I the boy who held his tongue beneath
    the honeysuckle blossoms
and spoke to trees before he
    could speak to humans.
And that sweetness is very specific.
It is that moment in the evening when we
stretch out together in our bed to relax
and suddenly you turn your head on the pillow
and look at me.
Your eyes become the fires
where my child heart warms itself
    and listens for the ancient tales.
This gaze
    arises beyond you
        and comes through you
           to me
        from all that is true and beautiful
        in woman loving man

calling back to what is beyond me
    and comes through me
        to you
    all that is true and beautiful
        in man loving woman.
Sweetness unimagined,
no artificial flavor or color,
no fine print.
Pure me.
    Pure you.
Full disclosure
        of the soul.

Short Selling
for Annie

You sell yourself short
even though you're five foot seven.
This would all cease if
you could see yourself
through my eyes…
How do I tell you?
You are more than a unique terrain
more than a luxuriant new planet
    or solar system,
more, even, than a universe.
These things can be studied
    known
    classified
by scientists
    even the most remote spaces and places
their physics, their temperatures and ages.
But you…
cannot be known in such a way
through micro or telescopes
or microwaves or light waves.
There is no way to classify
the shifting planes of your face
as your moods move from dark to light
and back again.
You are a mystery of beauty
    that cannot be unwound.
No categories can contain
how you turn the smallest space into art
with a tiny hand-painted box put here to hide a candle
and two small stone monkeys holding hands there
on which to balance thick, lovely cubes of soap;
the effort you are willing to exert to strip the front door
of its aged shuck
and renew it in a shade of blue

I've never seen on a door
so that when we approach and enter our house
we are moving within the frame of your imagination;
the effort you are willing to exert to haul just the right table
into our dining room so that
sitting in morning light
or evening
an impressionistic mist enfolds our hearts.
I have studied and studied you
how you encourage, love and celebrate me
and in turn receive my love
constantly creating new frames—both large and small--
to bring each moment to its ultimate expression.
Still, there are no frames or boxes that can be your boundaries.
You are a mystery of beauty
even in your anger
at your own imperfections and foolishness
as you gaze upon some aspect of your body
time and gravity are reshaping
for their own artful purposes.
Even in your raw fear
that we met too late
to have fifty or sixty years together,
even in this fear
you are a mystery of beauty.
And the truth is
    sixty years
    wouldn't be nearly enough
yet one day
    is far more
        than enough.
That is part of the mystery.
    That is part of the beauty.

Singularity
for Annie

When I heard physicists talking
    about just one universe
        emerging from
            a singularity
                smaller than a sesame seed
and then
    the possibility there are 10 to the 500 sesame seed universes
--the tiniest
    of germinating sources
        for virtually all possibilities—
and I do mean *all*, including
    worms and worm holes
            spiral staircases and spiral galaxies
    the eyes of storms
        and the eyes of butterflies,
    the tails of cats and comets,
        sunrises, sunsets, Sundays and sunburns…
not to mention
    the possibility of you and me
        as individuals
no less you and me together,
I have to be honest…
    my mind
        could barely
            brush these meanings
for all my stretching.
Nothing in my childhood
    prepared me for acres
        of white equations
            on blackboards.
Oh, I made my way through arithmetic
    all the way to algebra
across the street to geometry
    up the hill to trig,
        even managed

a leap
        to rocket trajectory
--mostly riding the enthusiasm of a few teachers
        for whom the alpha and omega
                were, well,
                        Alpha and Omega.
But far different matters
        (and matter matters to physicists more than most!)
...far different matters commanded my attention
        --the eclipse of leaf by leaf,
                the conundrum of smells in our cellar,
        the tails of raindrops wiggling across
                my bedroom window,
the black hole
        of our cat's pupils,
                the emergent fires
                        in the bodies of teenage
                                boys and girls
        and the halt in the time-space continuum
when strange animal sounds emanated from my parents bedroom
                as I temporarily paused
                        on my way
                from one dream to another.
But then
        we
sprang into being
        from nearly nothing,
                you and I
and I became a believer
        in ideas that do need
                acres of blackboards
                        to contain their proofs,
a believer that *nearly* nothing
        is actually very far from nothing itself
                especially when it contains
                        in its unnoticeable seed
the possibility

of everything--
　　all that we have become
　　and are becoming--
and the possibility
　　that we might never have happened
　　　　not a
　　　　single
　　　　thin-sliced
　　　　second
　　　　　of us
had a smattering of gravity
　　leaked out
　　　　and taken a one-way trip
　　　　　　to God knows where
(though physicists have told me
　　they are not in the business of God
unless he/she/it is a physicist
　　to which I say, why not?)

But, anyway,
　　in fact, we did…come into being
　　　　though mathematically
I'm unaware of anyone yet
　　having offered
　　a formula for human being…
but, anyway (*again!*)…
　　this "us" feels beyond the membrane
　　　　of the known universe.
In this one, ours,
　　we find that humans actually *can* fly
　　even when they're well beyond their youth!
In this one,
　　we've gone from a black pencil dot
　　　　on the universal sketch-pad
　　to fully-fleshed out living color.
In this one
　　all the dreams that didn't come true

      in prior universes
    in spite of heroic efforts
        do
without
    even
        trying
even though the odds are equal
    they might not...
    and even though
        the birth of our universe
depended on the death of
          many others.

So,
    now
as the moon rests its cheek
    on the far ridge
        and you yours on my chest
I find myself strangely comfortable
    with the songs of singularity
        physicists croon
    from room to room,
    and vow to listen
        as long as I can
and to love matter and energy
        both dark and light
        right up to the final second
when what has been us
        decides not to be
          any more
       and instead
        goes out as seeds
          to sow
            new fields
              among
            the unborn stars.

Enough Already!
for Annie

There I was
--a guy from sea level
trying to climb from 9400 to 12800 feet
just to see a mountain framed by
a pile of rocks the Incas had placed there
for that exact purpose.
Oh, sure, it was a lookout point as well
but they weren't required to frame
the mountain on the other side of the valley
with such esthetic perfection.
That was who they were at their essence
--giving the functional full flight.
Yes, I confess I definitely chewed too many coca leaves
and was cross-eyed and out of breath
and quite sure I could catch those two falcons overhead
if I just got a running start,
though I wasn't quite sure which was the real one.

There you were
--trying to get rid of a bad cold
so you'd have the option of chewing
too many coca leaves and getting cross-eyed
up a mountain so we could both see two of each other
and, yes, you definitely drank too much
    cough medicine
and were having an out-of-body experience
giddy in the restaurant
and not quite sure who ate your lunch
but it couldn't have been you.

Well, happily,
metabolism—the unsung worker bee of the body—
has deposited us back
on firm flat turf

beyond coca and dextromethorphan.
You can actually feel your hand grasp a fork
and deposit its delectable freight
on your tongue.
I, for my part, can actually see
just one of you now
and my darling
I'm not the least bit disappointed,
for the Inca's fusion
of function and form
is but an expression of a Creator
whose esthetics took flight
in your face
and the long lines of your arms.
One
of you
is more than enough
for me!

Dandelions, We
for Annie

We may look
    like ragged dandelions to others,
but in our own eyes
    each morning
        we are fresh new
            wheels of
                white gold seed
            eager and able to
        free ourselves
           on
              the slightest breeze
                    love can muster.

Love Doesn't Count
for Annie

How much do I love thee?
    I cannot count that high.
I tried...oh, I really tried
    and so did you.
We said we loved each other
    more than all the sunflowers
        in all the galaxies
            in all the universes.
Van Gogh smiled
    in his grave,
        still sucking on a brush, no doubt.
We said we loved each other
    more than all the sand on all the beaches
        of all the worlds
            ...everywhere,
and just in case there is a nowhere
    and it's actually somewhere,
        we included that in our calculation, too.
Raymond, the Rain Man,
    smiled and offered the exact number.
We declined.
What silliness is that?
Love is not math
    but if it were
its endless digits would have Pi
    groveling on its knees
        crying,
    "I'm not worthy!"

The Pointer
for Annie

It was just the two of us
   in the car
      and our sweet husky, Sofie,
         in the back…
I, the man of verses, driving
   and Leonard,
once the man of form and function,
     the passenger,
his left hemisphere,
where microscopic
gray-matter arches and balustrades
          once soared
   collapsed now into ruin.
Leonard, I'd been told,
had always liked to say,
   "Ideas and the images and words they ride
   only live when the blood is in them."
Since the stroke
   --no longer a metaphor
…no blood, no ideas, no images, no words
   or almost none;
      the few left him
   nothing more than knife scratches
     on an old drafting table.
Yes, he could ever so slightly
   expand their meanings
      by pointing with his left hand,
the right that had been his master tool
   and won a trophy case of
     architectural awards
   now not even a blunt instrument,
     more like a knob of wood
he might have placed at the bottom of a banister
     in a rustic home

             where such gnarl
        would serve as an aesthetic grace note.
Driving
    the two of us
    and Sofie
whose repertoire of deep-throated rumbles
                    seemed more complex
    than the utterances
of the man who had loved colonnades and cantilevers.
Driving
    through the jerry-rigged matrix
        of Southern California's highways.
Driving,
    Leonard relating in the simplest terms...
        a finger pointing to an old hotel,
an unusual church spire, an inventive period mall design,
    speaking one of the few words
he could still manage...
"bad," spoken with the A drawn out
    for the emphasis other words once gave...
    and "wonderful" spoken without the d...
        coming out as, "Wunnerfull"
and sounding
    not like the judgment of an accomplished man
        a man of nuance and knowledge
            but of a child
            with ice cream
        --sweetness on the tongue
            and in the tone
just as the stroke
    had softened
        his face
    from intellectual fierceness
        to enforced innocence
...yet even as I
    had often studied
        that boyish face

I kept seeing behind it
    an image I had witnessed in Berlin
        as a young man
--the half-bombed steeple of the church
    in the city's heart
        jabbing an incessant accusation
           at the sky.

I was glad I hadn't known him
    before.
        Before.
The word had more girth to it
    than ever.
It reeked with rot…the rot of a soul.
People who had been part of that "before"
    said, "This is not Leonard.
    Leonard was a kind and brilliant man,
though, yeah, probably too consumed by his work."
One side of my brain took it
    at face value.
        The other side,
           figuring from
    my own life
        and the stories
I'd gleaned about Leonard,
    knew it was more complicated…
kindness could sometimes be the easy way out
    and brilliance could be
        the blinding light off a snowdrift.
           So few things about people are
        just as they seem.
But I also knew
    I had the luxury of an inner dialogue
        of which Leonard was deprived
           …or from which he was free.
    So I preferred to define "before"
    as the man who got up at three in the morning

      to help his step-daughter
          work her way
      towards her own
      degree in the shapes of things
          to come.
    All in all
whatever his blessings, wounds, complexities
    Leonard had been a person
    and now,
        not so much as that.

Still, I couldn't stop wondering what
        my companion's inner experience was.
"Leonard, since the stroke…are your thoughts clear?"
    "Yes," he answered, nodding emphatically
because the word itself was not sufficient.
    Sometimes Leonard would mix up "yes" and "no"
        but right now there was no mix up.
"Is it just that you can't retrieve the words?"
    "Yes." More nodding.
"Do you dream, Leonard?"
    "Yes." Nodding again.
"Do you still dream of architecture? Do you see buildings?"
    "Yes." A single very emphatic nod.
"Are they sometimes buildings you designed before the stroke?"
    "Yes."
"..sometimes beautiful buildings by others…historical…contemporary?"
    "Yes."
"…sometimes imaginary buildings, buildings not yet built?"
    "Yes." The nodding continuing throughout.
    Then, after a pause, "Did you ever make it to Europe, Leonard?"
    "No." Emphatic head shake.
"That's such a shame. You'd have loved it. Notre Dame…what a miracle
    …took two hundred years to build!"
Tears in Leonard's eyes, followed by the fierce exclamation, "Bullshit!"
    …the only way he could express
      the cruelty of his never having walked in the great cathedral

    and the likelihood he never would,
not in Notre Dame or Chartres or the Louvre or Les Invalides
  or the master structures of Italy, Germany, Russia,
  Greece, India, China, North Africa, South America.

I was glad I hadn't grown dismissive
  of Leonard's alternating
    prattle and pantomime.
Perhaps I could feel this person
  who remained all the more
because for me, there had been no
  first-hand before.

Driving still
  through a long silence
    that turned deeper into itself
      till even the sound of the road dissipated
  and Sofie put her head down
      in the back seat to sleep
  and I wandered further
  into the unlit hallways of my darkest imaginings
  into Leonard's dreams
    and his paralysis
      his wordlessness
      his hopelessness
and wondered if his thoughts really were clear
  or if this was a form of benign delusion,
wondered about the moment when
  the hyperbaric oxygen treatment,
contrary to his doctor's prediction,
  sent a thread-thin line of light
    into a small apse
  of awareness within him
…what could that be like
  to go into surgery a master of your craft
    admired in your field
  and awaken

     slammed back against the
     spiked wall
        of
    an unimagined
       prison,
nearly everyone you knew running
    as fast and far away as possible
    ...and wondered, too, if now he had any feelings
    of jealousy
or at least bitter irony
    or simple sadness
about the fact that
    I was about to marry
    his former wife, Annie,
who had cared for him for twelve years
          and would continue to
with my willing support
    for the rest of his life
         ...when Leonard raised
    his left hand
      and pointed across the freeway
   through the rain
    and once again said,
"Wunnerfull", his tone lifting uncharacteristically
   on the last syllable.
I turned
   thinking it might be one more building
     with an interesting roof line
        or façade,
      but it was not a building.
This time
   a rainbow,
       or actually
   the basic shaft of a rainbow
  --seven of the most brilliant colors
    I had ever witnessed
in a lifetime of loving rainbows

    --red, orange, yellow, green, blue, indigo, and violet--
        each straight and clear as a stone pillar
      thrusting into the cupolas of winter clouds.
Leonard and I looked and looked
    and Sofie
        without a cue
            sat up and looked, too.
Miles of silence later
    with the colors
        in the rearview mirror
            I turned to my companion and said,
                "Thank you for the rainbow, Leonard."
                He
        patted my right hand
            with his left
                and nodded.

Four-Letter Love
for Annie

People say
they love their shoes
    or a movie,
        a book,
            their hairdresser
    a football team,
             their car
    or some celebrity.
I understand they like them…a lot.
    They get excited about them.
        Fine.
But they don't really love them.
Love may be
the most abused four-letter word
    in our language.
So let me be clear.
I really like that shirt you got for me,
    the white linen one that wears so well
        with the tails out.
I really like the yellow cymbidium you brought home.
It's presence changes the way I feel
    walking into the kitchen.
The things you did with our bathrooms,
    --the colors and fixtures--
        were all amazing and
    make me want to stay there
far longer than I should,
    especially when friends come by!
I like all these things and many more.
    They excite me.
But, darling, you are the only thing or person
    in this house
        I love
        … other than Sofie, our teddybear-coated husky.

        But I hope Sofie isn't listening because
           there is no comparison between those loves.
I adore her
   but I would not give my life for her.
I *would* give my life for you.
What's more important
(since that isn't likely to be put to the test)
   is that I give my life *to* you
   for you
      with four simple letters.
There's something perfect about
   the matching of such
      a state of being
  with only four scribbles.
  Don't ask me why
except that I remember turning four…
    I do,
     and feeling perfectly
   embraced by that number,
whereas three and five
   had too few
     or too many arms
   to form a perfect hug.
So I offer up
   my four-letter love
      in utter vulnerability
to become part of something
   never fully realized in my previous lives
--a vibrant and mischievous Us
   that can stand and dance on its own four feet
     with its own four arms
       holding itself
     in a tight little tango,
a love
that is better than me or you alone
   on our very best days in the past.

So let there be no doubt.
    Your spaghetti sauce
        is a world-class tongue-teaser
and your hat collection
    precious in all the looks it makes possible.
But I would never use
    the same word
to describe my appreciation of a sauce, a hat,
    a book, movie, shoe or basketball team
as I am compelled to use right now.
    I love you.
    I love Us.
    I love you in this Us.
    I love me in this Us.
We are in the lap of a goddess
    and her name
        should be spoken
far less often
    and even then,
        only
quietly,
    as close to silence
        as possible
            without being silent,
    like the sound
        of a pen
    forming four figures
        on a page.

Love Liberated
for Annie

Evening
    on the mountain,
three peaks aligned
    before me
        like the spread
            end feathers
                of an eagle's wing.
I am its body
    as I think of you,
        floating
            over the valley floor
toward the dunes
    and the sea
        and the farthest sky.

The Apprentice
for Annie

You are the one
with the post-doctoral degree
    in shopping—an intergalactic master
from another star system.
I am your humble apprentice.
Yes, I will venture out into the wilds of Costco
and Target with you.
I will carry my GPS so I don't fall into an enemy trap
as you charge ahead with your laser gaze firing,
    credit card at the ready.
I will sound the digital trumpet for each outrageous
buy you wrestle into the cart
with its tendrils flailing the air.
As you veer right, I will arc left.
Between the two of us,
our reconnaissance will be perfect.
We will do barrel rolls in our land-speeders
over the store floor and attack, attack, attack.
No four loaves for the price of one,
three bottles for the price of one,
two plants for the price of one
…or free snack
    will escape us.
When we have cleared checkout,
we will tap our communicators
and whisper, "Beam us up, Scotty.
We have hunted and harvested
in the heartlands of the
Costcotians and Targetanians.
Victory is ours!"
And during mission review
I will stand proudly
as you pin the medal on my chest
for bravery in the face of over-stimulation!

Spoonin'
for Annie

It must have been around five in the morning
when you pressed your breasts and belly to my back
and I thought, "Hmmmm,
I'm not going to get up now
and weld the axle on that old jalopy
…not that I know how to weld or have an old jalopy.
It's Saturday morning and maybe some guy does.
He's welcome to the work.
I'm not goin' anywhere."

You reached around and slid your hand over my chest
to my shoulder and down my arm to my fingers
and I thought, "Hmmmm,
I'm not going to get up now
and finish my essay on how to grow tomatoes
in a gravity-free environment
…since I haven't started that piece
    and have absolutely no clue how to.
It's Saturday morning and maybe someone does.
He or she is welcome to the work.
I, personally, am going nowhere."

I reached back around and slid my hand lightly over your hip
and thought, "Mmmmm, I'm not going hunting
…not that I know how or want to.
It's Saturday morning and the neighbor is probably headed out
to terrorize the county's turkeys.
He's welcome to that work.
I'm stayin' right here."

You rolled over and faced the other way.
I rolled over and spooned behind you,
feasting on your smells
and the texture of your skin,

wondering at how inviting your neck and shoulders are
of kisses, many kisses
    so many kisses.

And I thought,
"Hmmmm, there's a lot of stuff I could do, might do, should do
but can't or won't do
as long as you're here in bed with me.
All these people with their weekend 'honey-do' lists
--shooting off nail guns, lighting up table saws, mowers, cultivators, sprayers—
hey, c'mon!
It's Saturday morning!
What's with them?
They fell in love,
    courted for months,
wanted nothing more than to spend
hours naked nibbling on each other
and scribbling love poems,
spent way too much on a wedding
    bought their first house
    started raising kids
worked their butts off all week
every week
    for what?
For the thrill of firing up power tools?
Well, they can keep their routers, band saws,
leaf blowers and barbecues.
Our needs are simpler.
Our technology, too.
We are the implements of our mutual desire.
I am a spoon.
My Annie is a spoon
and our bed is a drawer slot
    till late
        this afternoon!"

Church Whispers
for Annie

In the stone church
the choir conjured tapestries
    of Sixteenth Century
        sound.
"I don't really like this," you whispered.
"It's pretty enough," I answered,
    "but not my favorite either—harmonious
        but not melodic."
You leaned into my shoulder and said,
"But I sure like you."
"And I sure like you," I answered.
"We're harmonious
    and melodic…"
"Yes," you added, "with an occasional dissonance,
    just for mischief's sake."
We rested our temples on each other's
    and I said, "Uh-huh.
We're definitely
    a
    Twenty-First Century
        tune."

Knowing and Knowing
for Annie

The truth is
    I've always known you.
It was you hiding behind the rhododendron
    beneath the dining room window
        wasn't it?
I was three or four
    in winter
and the snow falling from the roof
    brought you
        to my attention.
And in spring
    it was your laughter wreathing the dogwood blossoms
    and then scampering away
        --a mischievous butterfly.
It was you sitting beside me on the curb
    as I launched stick boats in the rumbling rain
    and sang them off to indescribable adventures
...then you with your hand invisibly on mine
    as I tried to describe those adventures anyway,
rolling words together in ways
    I had only just imagined
        at that very second
    as I felt you, knew you
        with your small girlish body
        and your big love.
Of course it was you...
as surely as it was me standing just behind
    your square little shoulder
        as you stood on the stool after dinner washing dishes
        listening to the kids play down in the street;
and me beside you as you
    wandered into a gallery
    to study the paint drippings of a man
    whose name would mean nothing
        till years later,

and me touching your fingers as your hands
made their own first designs on paper,
    me in awe
    as you found ways to roll colors together
    you had only just imagined at that very second
    as you felt me, knew me.
Of course, it was me.
It was me crying with you in the night
    both of us loved,
      though not enough,
        both of us too alone,
both of us yearning for the other to physically appear,
    believing with all our hearts
    it was just a matter of
      taking one step in the right direction
    or turning around fast enough
    to break through the field of all possible realities
    to the only one that mattered
    the one
    that would put us materially side by side
    never to leave.

Well, my darling…it took a while, didn't it?
We could say it was unfair we had to wait so long,
    but then there was much to learn,
    each of us finding the full breadth
    of what it would mean to stand naked
    in each other's eyes
      to know life's beauty and ferocity
    coincidence and paradox
      fragility, bitterness and bliss
--all rolled together
    as utterances and colors
we could not have imagined
    until this very breath we are taking
      together.

There
for Annie

Annie, look

   ...the osprey,

      reason enough for a sky!

Remedy
for Annie

It is a strange time and scape we are walking.
The wind is strong.
    The echoes of the old gods have been swept
        off mountain tops
           and faraway beaches.
    Fire from the tall trees
        singes earth and sky.
But come
my sweet soul,
    into the river we go.
Here we will make our stand
immersed to the tops of our heads
    in the foolishness
        of romance.

Half Moon
for Annie

The moon is flat on its back
    staring into the darkness,
its light wasted
    on the waves below.
Forlorn
    the moon
        forlorn
till her lover
    the sun
        returns.

World-Walker
for Annie

You are tough as nails
and soft as sage blossoms.
You can burn or bless me with a look.
Out of that same glance
    peers a child of three
        too innocent to do either.
Within your body
    a woman of thirty makes her nest
and lures me to it.
Sometimes in the pursing of your lips
    I hear the song of a crone
        whose wisdom
    humbles the ages.
You are baudy, outrageous, profane,
mercurial and elegant,
    unsteady, anxious
yet
    sure and calm as an ancient oak.
You suspect people of the worst,
despise and curse them
yet pound the sky on their behalf,
enfold and befriend them,
    kneel in their pews,
empty your pockets into theirs.
Between these poles
you travel all roads,
    eat at all tables
sit in every chair.
Your feet
    are covered with dust.
Come.
    Let me wash them for you
        so you can walk anew
    into the world
...but this time
    with me at your side.

The Question
for *Annie*

In your eyes
I see silk scarves moving in a breeze
...that same breeze
    throwing light
        on the surface of a pond
from whose shadowed depths
    fins swirl and push silently against the water.
What is this love
    --light,
        liquid,
            silk,
                flesh
                      or air?

Summer in Autumn
for Annie

It's tempting
to refer to ours
as love in autumn
since we are certainly beyond
what passes for the middle years.
But if there is a season
prevailing within us
it's summer.

In our world,
the lawns are not newly seeded.
They've filled out.
The apple and apricot
aren't blooming.
They're fruiting.
The robin isn't warming its eggs.
They've hatched.
The sun is high,
the days long,
though swift,
but then,
they were swift
when we hopscotched and bicycled
our way through childhood
June, July and August
arriving too soon
at a new school year.

There is ripening.
We have seeded and cultivated
each other
pinched and pruned,
fed and tended
touched our fingertips to

each other's bare branches
to call forth leaves,
leaves to call forth buds,
buds to call forth fruit,
gently bound each other's hearts
with vines whose fragrance
permeates
the warm air.

The only reds and yellows
are the skins of apples, peaches, berries
and the crisp flesh of watermelon.
Autumn may be studying
across the street
but she'll have a long wait
if we have anything
to say about it.

July Skies
for Annie on the 2ⁿᵈ anniversary of our meeting

July skies
…in childhood
the bluest blue
by day
unreachable
yet
the source
of white balls whacked from bats
over the greenest grass
whacked so hard and high
their lowly births
forgotten in a blink
emerging from
points far above the neighbors' houses;
my body spurred to action
    the long muscles ever longer
and gloved right hand
bigger than my gloveless father's
stretched out beyond me
to catch those stars
escaping night for day.

July skies
…in childhood
the grayest blue
by dusk
unfathomable
yet the backdrop and the source
of fireflies
turning on and off
their tiny bursts of dawn
even as their masters and mothers
emerged far above
as lions, dragons, hunters,
    bearers of water.

My small hand
grown large
against my face
cradled for a moment
a thousand blinking suns
escaping day for night.

July skies
...their images and essences
unchanged for decades,
no subsequent moment
big enough to nudge aside
the lilt and clarity of childhood
until you,
you standing in the doorway
on the twenty-seventh day of the seventh month
in the two thousand and seventh year
offering your entire soul in a single kiss.
Stars and suns
left their homes for good,
nestled between my hands and yours
till we tossed them out one by one
to light the way ahead.
And so we've traveled the mundane world,
and so we've traveled the holy world
and so we will continue
marking the passage each July
with sky-gazing and soul-kissing
    till all our stars and suns are used
        and midnight blue is upon us.

About the Author

Bob Kamm was born in New York City in 1947, the youngest of three sons. His father, Herb, was a journalist, his mother, Phyllis, a free lance writer. The open territory was poetry and that's where Bob began staking his claim at a young age.

Throughout his childhood in the suburban New Jersey town of Summit, and throughout his travels as a young man across the US, Europe and the Middle East, he continuously worked his craft. When he entered the business world in his mid-twenties, he was well served by his ability to represent himself with eloquence on paper and on his feet. But there was something far more important to him—his son. Bob was a single dad in the late 70's and early 80's when there was little understanding and even less support for such a role. He put aside career ambitions for several years so he could be a real and present father.

Eventually, as his son matured, Bob was able to devote more time to his career. By the end of the 1990's, he had gained wide recognition as an inspirational business innovator, consultant and speaker exhorting the world of commerce to make ethics its central organizing force.

As he focused increasingly on leadership development and change management, his clients came to include individuals and organizations in show business, the healthcare and legal professions, Olympic competition, real estate, automobile manufacturing and sales, the hospitality industry, architecture, construction, law enforcement, psychotherapy, writing, a variety of retail businesses and non-profits.

In 2000, he published his first book, *The Superman Syndrome: Why the Information Age Threatens Your Future and What You Can Do About It*. Drawing on his years of experience in the business world, he explored the costs of living at speed rather than depth, and suggested real-world remedies.

In 2002, he released his second book, Real *Fatherhood—the Path of Lyrical Parenting*. While this work chronicled Bob's personal experience as a single dad, it could well serve as a primer for parents in all the diverse family settings of our time.

As a result of these first two publications, Bob appeared on CNN, Fox, NBC and numerous other media outlets.

In 2007, Bob fully came home to himself, publishing *Lyric Heart, Poems and Other Musings*. This collection includes work across decades Bob produced even as he was raising his son and building a career.

In July of 2007, Bob and Andrea met. They fell for each other hard, fast and certain. So began the new cycle of poems which comprise this book.

Bob and Andrea are married and live in San Luis Obispo, California where they offer therapy and workshops for singles, couples and parents at the *San Luis Relationship Institute* which they founded in 2009. The Institute also offers coaching for leaders at all levels of organizational development—community non-profit, business and government. Andrea is a Licensed Marriage & Family Therapist, a Board Registered Clinical Art Therapist, a Certified Advanced Imago Therapist and a Certified Imago Workshop Presenter, in addition to holding certifications in a number of other therapeutic disciplines. Bob is a Certified Imago Educator and Certified Imago Workshop Presenter as well as a thirty-five year veteran of the business world.

Oh yes…he's still writing poems for Annie.

Discover more at: www.loveover60.com
www.slrii.com
www.bobkamm.com

Made in the USA
Lexington, KY
06 January 2017